Leonardo da Vinci
Man - Inventor - Genius
is a production of Event Marketing Service GmbH
Geusaugasse 9, 1030 Vienna / Austria

www.event-marketing.com

Publisher: C&E Productions and Publishing, Danzingerstr. , 2523 Tattendorf
Editorial office: Mag. Christoph Rahofer
Author: Dipl. Ing. Reinhard Fink
Cover design: Constanze Necas
Photos of the exhibition and layout: © David-Atelier www.david-atelier.de

© of the texts by the author, © of the photos and sketches see image register

Models were built by Niccolai, Linner and Event Marketing Service GmbH

The use of the sketches by kind permission of Reprint - Verlag - Leipzig
(www.reprint-verlag-leipzig.de)
Title: Dr. Hermann Grothe - Leonardo da Vinci als Ingenieur und Philosoph - 1874

Printed at: Lindauer Druckerei, Eschbaumer GmbH & Co, Germany

ISBN-10: 3-9502004-1-X
ISBN-13: 978-3-9502004-1-6

www.leonardo-da-vinci.us

Dear friends of Leonardo da Vinci,

Like so many others in the last couple of years, the "Leonardo-enthusiasm" caught me completely unexpected. What sparked this curiosity was the reading of the "Da Vinci Code" by Dan Brown. I wanted to know more about his true background, what interested him, who he was as a person, in essence, who the man Leonardo Da Vinci really was. Like one of those "flukes", which were a major contribution to Robert Langdon in his investigations, good friends of mine gave me additional insight into literature concerning Leonardo da Vinci, transforming holidays taken with my family in Italy into explorations of the life of Leonardo.

In addition I became friends with an Italian craftsmen-family from Florence who committed themselves to the reproduction of replications of Leonardo Da Vinci's inventions. A passion the Niccolai family has pursued for already two generations. After a lot of meticulous research and investigations into means of production, the culmination of this collection of Leonardo's enormous and prolific body of work is finished and constitutes the largest touring exhibition of Leonardo da Vinci's inventions to date. More than 60 of his most innovative constructions are replicated by different specialized craftsmen to scale, based on the original drawings and manuscripts of the Codices, showcasing their functionality and efficiency. Computer simulations developed together with the University of Applied Arts in Vienna, Austria, additionally show the impact of physics, geometry, aerodynamics and a number of other fields in science interactively applied to make Leonardo's inventions work. It is important for me to depict Leonardo da Vinci from another perspective, finding a neutral point of view and avoiding the speculations about other, ulterior motivations of his work. With a summary of quotes by and about Leonardo, this book seeks to shed an additional and palpable insight into his life and his genius.

I hope you will find the same inspiration and pleasure as our team of scholars did through the realisation of this exhibition, and I want to personally thank all the partners, sponsors and friends of Leonardo da Vinci for their support.

Cordially yours,

Mag. Christoph Rahofer, producer

österreichisches
patentamt

Large causes, large effects

Patents, brands and designs, this is the tapestry which showcases the accumulation and inspiration of numerous inventions and innovations that are a crucial part of the human intellect, and at the same time act as an archive for the motivation and ultimately the prosperity of future generations. The increasing competition between companies makes it more and more important to legally protect investments in products and service. Thereby it is important to protect the name of a company and products against counterfeiting. Access to limited information means a competitive advantage.

The increasing globalisation of market systems, shorter cycles of innovation as well as rising development costs for new products pose a special challenge for small and medium companies. The increase in manufacturing flexibility has spawned the proliferation of new and innovative products and services. This flexibility, being market driven, has meant that the production and manufacturing of goods and services is globally determined, driven largely by the cheapest means of production, where infrastructure for research and development, as well as the basic conditions of production are realized at a relatively low cost. For this reason, global competition by the major economic powers of Japan, the USA and Europe are at the same time in contention about patents and licences. Simply being able to provide a service is not enough to compete within the complex intertwining of macro market economics. Patents, licences and intellectual property rights are an essential component to modern business protocol and success. In accordance, the volume of the patents sought and awarded has shown a constant increase over the last couple of years. The increase in patents is a reflection of the importance of research and development as a key factor in economic growth and prosperity. Finding an agreeable diversity within macro market systems is the motto of the EU, and is expressed through the declaration of a unified constitution. Unified European patents, patents for computer software, the reflection of all day work in national patent offices, the patent attorneys with their data bases of the 128 `member states of the World Intellectual Property Organization (WIPO), are being overshadowed by the complexity that arises from patents that are international in scope. As the number of people seeking patents increases, the demand for reorganisation of

patent documents and structures/infrastructures are imperative. Currently in Vienna, we are being bombarded with increased patent claims as well as in Munich, Paris, Washington, Tokyo, Peking and Brasilia.

The Austrian Patent Office, which supports and manages both in past and present eavors has remarkable resources - now going far beyond historical description - not only in regards to patent affairs, but as well in relation to industrial property rights, and wishes to contribute with joy and enthusiasm to this exhibition. This support is both in relation to the subject-related retrospective investigations of the genius of Leonardo Da Vinci, as well as to his interest in efficiency and the public-related scope of his inventions and services.

"I want to work wonders", wrote Leonardo as a young man. In the Renaissance there was a large number of artists, musicians, scientists, architects, engineers, inventors, and philosophers, but only Leonardo Da Vinci embodied all these disciplines simultaneously. He epitomised the universal genius and would hardly begin one project before immersing himself into another one. He had an endless number of fantasies, inventive ideas and above all visions for the future. He once said, "Who ever quotes authority in a discussion is not using his brain, he is using his memory." Leonardo, a figure who embodies the paradigm of the Renaissance, used his intellect to envision future possibilities, which in turn has helped to formalize the world in which we are currently living. Confucius, actually Kong Qui, the Chinese philosopher had made similar claims almost 2000 years previous to that of Leonardo: "Who does not think about the future will soon face big problems." We don't know if Leonardo Da Vinci ever read Confucius, but he as well lived and shared his concerns.

Dr. Friedrich Rödler

President of the Austrian Patent Office

LEONARDO

LEONARDO THE INVENTOR

Airborne transportation

table of contents

The life of Leonardo da Vinci transpired during one of the most moving and creative eras of mankind. With the "Renaissance" Europe left behind the "dark" years of superstition which dominated the Middle Ages. The downfall of Konstantinopel in 1453 by the Turks furthered the exportation of antique knowledge to Italy. The access to original texts from Platon, Aristoteles or Galen was now much more accessible, making possible the "rebirth of the antiquity" known as the "Renaissance". The consequence was the genesis of a new way of thinking which questioned tradition and emphasized curiosity and a thirst for knowledge, becoming integral qualities to one's pursuits. This experiment transformed into a legitimate tool and means to prove theoretical knowledge. This was the cultural medium for spirits like Leonardo da Vinci. "The Renaissance was the most progressive upheaval mankind had experienced; a time which asked for giants and created giants, colossus in thinking, in passion

The Human

Leonardo da Vinci

and moral courage, "in many-sidedness and erudition. At that time there existed not a more significant man, who did not do long travels, who did not speak several languages and who did not shine in different disciplines, 'Uomo Universale', against restrictions and specialization." "The heroes at his time were not oppressed by the divisiveness of specialized work. They lived in a daily practical struggle of synchronized disciplines - through the bounty and power of their mental courage, which made them into complete persons, theorists being the exception...". This time spawned a new job title, the "artist engineer". Engineer was synonymous with "brainstorming and clever ideas". This new mentality was supported less by the church and more by the bourgeoisie like the "Medici family" in Florence, who gained political influence and prosperity through trade endeavors. The culmination of the disciplines of art, techniques and science were expressed and found in Leonardo da Vinci, who expressed this symbiosis in its highest form, like never before and never after.

"In innumerable things he was centuries ahead of his contemporaries."

Charles Singer

Vinci - is a small village in the Tuscany, about 20 miles away from Florence. A wonderful landscape comprised of vineyards, olive groves, whirling brooks and pines - corn, and fruits and nuts. Born in 1452, Leonardo lived there until he was 13 years old.

pic.1 landscape near Vinci

pic.2 birthplace of Leonardo

pic.3 Vinci

pic.4 view of the roofs of Vinci

pic. 5 bust of Leonardo

... Leonardo was not a man of exaggerated claims:

...He was living off of bred, eggs, vegetables, mushrooms and fruits. Rarely did he drink wine, because of its revenge on the "drinker". He was a vegetarian.

...He lived an elegant lifestyle, always having the services of a butler and horses.

...In his lifetime he was regarded as a whimsical and curious person. There is nothing known about his relationships with women.

...Leonardo was a tall, strong, sportive man with a nice figure, symmetrically composed, graceful and with a striking appearance. He wore a short cloak. His hair, stylish and cultivated, fell in curly splender down to the middle of his breast...

...He spent most of his youth enjoying life and having a great time.

...Some researchers believed Leonardo was a homosexual, at least in his youth. This fact has shown to be something difficult to prove, and as a result this type of investigation was closed.

...The principles of his life can be illustrated by the following words of Leonardo:

> "The wish to learn is in all noble men's nature."
> "Experience is the source of all knowledge."
> "All our knowledge is based on perception."
> "A painter who knows no doubt will reach little."
> "Study the science of art and the art of science."
> "Mens sana in corpore sano."
> "All things and phenomenons are connected to each
> other."

pic.6 the birth certificate of Leonardo

Leonardo was the illegitimate son of a notary and a farmergirl from Vinci.

Leonardo's mother wasn't invited to attend his christening.

"I was presented with a grandson, the child of Sir Piero, my son, on the 15th of April, Sunday, at three o`clock at night. He was given the name Leonardo. The priest Piero di Bartolomeo baptized him, the godfathers were...."
(notice of his grandfather)

pic.7 Florence, Ponte Vecchio

"...there was something overtly-European and secretive about him, as with anyone who has had too many good or bad experiences."
Friedrich Nietsche

Leonardo

...After the plague-epidemic the number of inhabitants of Florence decreased from 40,000 to almost half. The prosperity of the city was based on the production of wollen material and the commerce system with 33 major banks. Leonardo served an apprenticeship there with Verrocchio and lived for about 24 years in Florence.

...The sculptor, goldsmith and painter Verrocchio, one of the most well known masters in Florence was the owner of one of the most prestigious artist's studios, the name of which was "Bottegas". Leonardo was his apprentice.

...In the first year Leonardo was schooled in drawing, which included how to make brushes and color pigments, how to mix colors, preparing the background, and methods for the application of gold leaf.

... The brushes were made out of the hair of an ermelin's tail, the stronger ones being composed out of pigbristle.

pic.8 Verrocchio

pic.9 Florence

..."The embarrassingly difficult struggle with his work, the seemingly limited escape from himself coupled with his indifference towards his own fate, this behaviour shows Leonardo's extremes."

Sigmund Freud

Leonardo and Florence

... In 1445 Johannes Gutenberg invents the letterpress with movable letters, referred to as the "Black Art".

... Gutenberg dies poor, his studio is distressed, his patents are worthless.

... The bible from Gutenberg is still the best example of a letterpress masterpiece from this time period.

... This was the beginning of a new era, the era of communication - Leonardo's time.

..."The Dekameron" marks the first masterpiece of European prose writing. (Hesse)

... It was a book about "the art to live" and a kaleidoscope of human passions, both satiric and frivolous.

... a lively testimonial of the bright Italian renaissance.

... "devoted also to the lovely women, who carry the flames of love, afraid and full of shame within their bosoms." (Boccaccio)

..."The Divine Comedy", a trip through hell, purgatory and paradise marks the most famous other world trip in world literature. (first printed in 1472)

...After his own projects failed, Dante held an office as a "political critic" and complained about the desolate conditions of Italy.

..."the most noble task of any politican consists of "guiding men to what is good, to what is god." (Dante)

pic.10 Florence

... the persecution and hunting of heretics, of "nonbelievers", was booming. In 1487 the inquisition in Spain began.

...most of the time the aim of the trials of the inquisition were to reach a sentence that would convict the defendant to death, being less about judging innocence and more about blame.

...names of witnesses and denunciators were undisclosed.

...witches were held responsible for thunder-storms, the death of livestock and diseases, were claimed to have had sexual intercourse with the devil and to have ridden on brooms.

...all defendents, most of them women, were tested with a simple water test: if the chained accused drowned, they were innocent, if they could swim, they had a pact with the devil and were incinerated.

pic.11 Baldung, two witches

Notices out of a protocol of a burning of witches in 1505:

..."Barbara admitted to having borrowed from one women 15 cents and from another one 8 cents. When the women asked for their money back, she bewitched them with a crippling pain."

...in addition she confessed an alliance with the devil..."

..."No, I do not admit all that. I confessed it under terrible tortures..."

...meanwhile the hangman had gathered together the wood for the stake and prepared the seat, seated himself, see sawed on it to prove he had fixed it right. The woman on the cart bit her lips together, but then started laughing, until she was shaking...

...the hangman untied the woman, pushed her to the seat on the stake and prepared her clothes...

...before the fire was lit, the priest said:" Dear woman, if the fire is lit, you have to scream devotionally in a loud voice...."My lord, take pity on me...". And so she did, screaming as long as she could in the consuming heat and smoke.

witches and stakes

pic.12 the young Leonardo

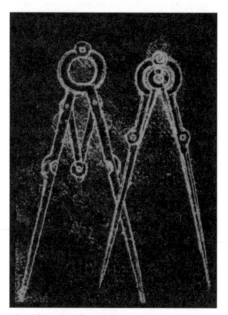

pic.13 pair of compasses belonging
to Leonardo

Education of Leonardo

..."I know that I am not a well read person. To an arrogant man it might be right to call me a man without erudition. Foolish people! It seems they don't know... that I took my teachings less from other people's words than from experiences.."

Before his apprenticeship, Leonardo had a school-education of a typical craftsman or salesman, with the main emphasis being mathematics. His whole life he struggled from his lack of Latin knowledge. When he was 50 years old, he began to learn Latin.

Leonardo owned a least 116 books: 54 of them were the works of scientists, 7 were written by technicians, 25 were Western literature, 14 were about religious or moral themes, and 16 of them were about the Latin language , grammar and vocabulary.

...because of his huge lack of understanding of the Latin language, it is probable that Leonardo did not read all the books he owned himself. With the translation of Euklid, his friend Pacioli most likely helped.

Leonardo gained most of his knowledge from conversations and through hearsay, while he was at court or at the university.

Symbols of computations:

...computational statements were still just verbal until this time. In 1489 the symbols + and - were used for the first time.

...notations of high numbers were introduced:

-million
-billion
-trillion

...the changeover from Roman to Arabic letters pushed through (Adam Riese)

Leonardo`s time:

`
... In 1490 invention of flint glass

... In 1497 tobacco plants reach Europe

... In 1500 the use of pencils

... In 1465 printing of scores

... In 1502 invention of the first pocket watch "Nürnberger Ei"

... Forks were used in rich families - conditioned by the fashion of the times: the ruffle

"The infinite contours of Leonardo`s being you will forever just divine from a distance."
Jakob Burckhardt

"...his talent was so immense and natural in a way that what ever he was interested in, he resolved with the greatest of ease the most difficult things."
Vasari

„done for the first time"

... "the medici clan" held the authority in Florence. A family of salespersons, bankers, tax accountants and popes, they supported artists and theorists.

...Lorenzo de Medici, called "il magnifico" over saw applications to the studio of Verocchio. He was Leonardo's master.

...Lorenzo recommended Leonardo to the court of the Sforzas to Milan, as a decorator for parties.

pic.14 Giuliano dei Medici 1478 (Botticelli)

..."the Medicis made me big and destroyed me." (Leonardo)

... In 1482 Leonardo wrote a letter to Ludovico Sforza, duke of Milan and provided him with his service.

...30 out of 36 skills he performed there were technical skills.

...Ludovico Sforza, called "il moro", was an ample patron of the arts and put Leonardo to service for 18 years.

pic.15 Ippolito de Medici 1533 (Tizian)

"In our changing Italy, where nothing is fixed and no traditional governance exists, menials can be kings." (contemporary about the rise of the Sforza family in Milan)

Medici and Sforza

www.event-marketing.com

VENICE ...was at this time with its 160.000 inhabitants the "head of Italy", with a solid political system and thriving economy. The richness of Venice grew through its maritime trade and industry. The production of glass and silk and the letterpress came to the fore.

...when he was 48, Leonardo spent a year together with his friend Luca Pacioli, a mathematician, in Venice.

...Luca Pacioli pioneered work in mathematics.

... His book about the golden section was illustrated by his friend Leonardo.

...Tizian came at the age of 10 years from the Dolomite Alps to Venice.

...He was really efficient and ruthless in defending his domain. He quickly became the official government sanctioned painter of Venice.

...Tizian visited Michelangelo in Rome, who influenced him greatly.

pic.16 Venice about 1496 (Bellini)

pic. 17 Venice

Venice

Leonardo about talkers

…"Truly, some talkative and unreasoning people should characterize themselves just like the passage for food, a person, who increases refuse, and as a filler of cesspits, because nothing else in the world will be bared to them, because nothing good will be done from them, because nothing will remain from them than cesspits."

…"Demetrius used to say that there was no difference between the words and speech of the unskilled and ignorant and the sounds and rumblings caused by the stomach being full of superfluous wind. This he said, not without reason, for, as he held, it did not in the least matter from what part of them the voice emanated, whether from the lower parts or the mouth, since the one and the other were of equal worth and importance."

…"There is something, which the more despised, the more necessary it is, and that is the advice; which are not willingly heard by those, who are in need of it, and are the unaware."

… „Patience serves as a protection against wrongs as clothes do against cold. For if you put on more clothes as the cold increases it will have no power to hurt you. So in like manner you must grow in patience when you meet with great wrongs and they will then be powerless to vex your mind."

…"Beware of the teachings of those gamblers, whose considerations are not proved by experience."

pic.18 Beatrice d'Este (Leonardo)

...Women were working in the house, tilling the fields and caring for their families. They were expected to be reserved and modest.

...They had to succumb to the will of men, who had the right to use force if necessary.

..."I tell you men, don't beat your wives when they are pregnant... I'm not saying you are not allowed to beat them ever, but choose the right time" (a preacher).

...Just really rich women or women from an orden could avoid these conditions.

...In the Renaissance prostitution was accepted and institutionalized.
"Prostitution keeps men away from homosexuality... and protects women from molestation".

...In Rome arose the courtesan profession, an alternative to prostitution and to marriage. The courtesan was a woman who offered sexual compliances as well as satisfied musical, literary and other cultural demands at the same time. Her attributes were the lap dog and the lute.

pic.19 Porträit of a woman (Leonardo)

womens destiny

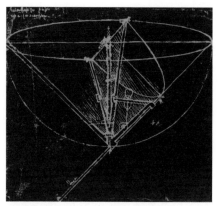

pic.20 construction of an ellipse
(Leonardo)

"These days I have read the book by Leonardo da Vinci about painting and understand now why I could never understand such things."

Goethe

...Kopernikus declared: "All planets, as well the earth, circle the sun - she is the center of universe". ...In 24 hours the earth rotates once around its own axis and within one year once around the sun.

...Opposition by the church. Luther about Kopernikus: "This fool wants to invert the whole art of astronomy".

..."Money against sins" - In 1517 Luther, the reformer, appears before the public with his 95 theses against the selling of indulgences.

...The split of the church into Catholic and the Protestant was the result of "the reformation".

...In 1521 Luther translated the bible into German.

Leonardo`s way of working

...Leonardo's thirst for knowledge coupled with his educational background resulted in his ability to rethink existing questions from their origins. With all things he was rigorous, spontaneous and unprejudiced.

...Leonardo was a pracitcal man, who was seeking practical solutions. For him science was just a tool of the trade.

...He wrote almost exclusively using a mirror, most likely in order to hide his thoughts from others, including the ascending class of society. Lots of the things he thought or did were forbidden. Leonardo was also left-handed. His writing methodology changed over the years, adapting to what was appropriate given the subject and the addressee.

...Leonardo left behind an immense body of work with more then 100,000 drawings on approximately 6,000 pages.

...Just 17 of his painting still exist, some of them still unfinished.

pic.21 Mona Lisa (Leonardo)

"...Painting meant so little to him, that you can see it as a small part in the overall diction of a universal genius. He used it casually, when he didn't have more important things to do..."
Bernhard Berenson

... In 1477 the Earl Dracula dies a natural death in Transylvania at the age of 46.

... Dracula was well known for his exceptional cruelness against his enemies.

... Nostradamus, a French doctor gave all his attention to battling against pestilence.

...When his practice wasn't going well, he established an observatory, becoming a clairvoyant and publishing his prophecies.

...His real name was Philippus Aureolus Theophrastus Bombastus von Hohenheim. Out of protest he called himself "Paracelsus".

...He was a doctor and professor. Due to his unconventional methods for treatment, he alienated many people and had to live a vagrant life as a charlatan.

...He had confidence in natural medications as well as in chemical substances like quicksilver and sulfur and believed in that all lives were influenced by the universe.

"...that arise these magical inapprehensible and unthinkable miracle-men, whose most beautiful expression [...] among artists is Leonardo da Vinci."
Friedrich Nietzsche

Dracula-Nostradamus-Paracelsus

"Maybe there is in the whole world not another example of such a universal, creative mind, who was at the same time so unable to please himself, so full with desire for infinity, so naturally evolved, so far ahead of his century and the following. His figure expresses inconceivable sensibility…"
Hippilyte Taine

...In 1492 Columbus discovered America, "the new world" for the Europeans. Columbus failed to have anything to show from this discovery.

...The discovery of America cost 2 million maravedis, which was at this time the average income per month of a Spanish Duke.

...In 1521 Magellan did the first circum navigation of the world in 1,100 days.

...Just 18 out of 265 men came back from this trip, himself losing his life.

...This was the proof that the earth is a sphere.

land in sight...

pic.22 Cathedral of Milan

In Milan the industry was booming, in particular the production of weapons and fine drapery. In Milan there were about 70,000 inhabitants. Leonardo resided there for about 23 years and was in service of the court of the "Sforza-Family".

Letter of congratulations from Leonardo to his brother given the birth of his brother's son:

"My dearly loved brother!

Today just a few short lines, to say that I received a letter from you, which exclaimed you have an heir. About that you were extremely lucky. Well, when I took you for an intelligent man, that I am now absolutely clear in my mind, that I have a lack of judging right like you have a lack of intelligence. You were lucky that you created for yourself a sympathetic enemy, who will aspire with all his power to gain freedom, which he will get not before your death".

The brother of Leonardo

..."Try to keep your health and that will work so much the better to help you stay away from doctors."

..."Everybody is trying to acquire property, just to spend later on doctors, the destroyers of life. Therefore doctors have become rich."

pic.23 Farmer at the dentist (J.Liss 1616)

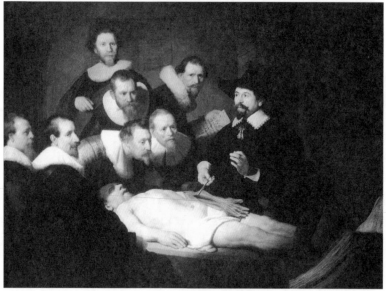

pic.24 The Anatomy Lesson of Dr. Tulp (Rembrandt)

... One third of all children died from influenza, measles or under nourishment before they had their first birthday.

...The lung was thought to be a heart-cooling sponge, the liver as source of the urine, the breast milk as restrained blood of menstruation.

... Pestilance, leprosy, syphilis, and malaria were the most dangerous diseases at this time.

...Syphilis was medicated with quicksilver.

… **Charles d'Amboise**, governor of Louis XII in Milan, asked Pier Soderini, the head of government of Florence, many times to extend the leave of Leonardo. Soderini replied angrily to Charles:

„... I do not concede one more day of vacation, because Leonardo was not acting like he should act in taking a high sum of money in exchange for performing a great work. But he gave the work only its beginning...

…and he is giving of himself already like a traitor."

...Charles to Soderini full with commendation for Leonardo: "...we should admit being among them, who loved him, before you knew him. But since we know him we see, that his famous name for paintings, is meek in comparison to the commendation he deserves for the other things, in which he is giving all his capability".

Isabella d'Este is begging the General Vicar of Florence to asked Leonardo to make a painting for her. Isabella to the Vicar:

"...and if he would be reluctant, just try to convince him to make a small tablet with the madonna on it..."

Vicar to Isabella: "... to me the life of Leonardo seems to be unbalanced and so undefined that he is living just from one day to the other..."

"...he has put much work into geometry and with the paint-brush he is very impatient..."

the female ideal

"In some things the great Leonardo stayed all his life a little bit infantile; you can say, that all great men have to stay a bit childlike. He was still playing when he was an adult and because of that to some contemporaries he was weird and inapprehensible."

Sigmund Freud

...Small mouth, long neck, golden hair, plucked eyebrows and skin like porcelain.

...External beauty was considered as a sign of inner moral perfection.

...For them, who were under privileged by nature exists herbal fragrances.

...An outstanding attribute at this time was the artificiality.

...Boccaccio wrote: "the barbers are maltreating the women, they pick their eyebrows and shave their forehead."

...Short and triangular veils were popular to young women, the older ones prefered shoulder-length square veils.

pic. 25 woman by Leonardo

..."Jacomo moved to me at the day of Magdalena in 1490, at the age of 10 (thievish, false, defiant, cormorant)." (Leonardo was calling him later "Salai", devil).

..."Caterina came on the 16th of July in 1493.

..."The 14th of March in 1494 Galeazzo came to me on condition that I give him 5 Lira per month for his alimony, to pay on the 15th every month. His father gave me two Rhenish Guilders."

..."Tomorrow in the morning, the 2nd of January 1496, you have to fix the belt and try it on.

..."I note that I, Leonardo da Vinci, gave on the 8th of April 1503 four golden ducats to the painter Vante. Salai brought it by hand and handed it out himself. He said he will give it back in between 40 days."

..."On the 24th of September 1513 I traveled together with Giovanni, Francesco di Melzi, Salai, Lorenzo and the Fanfoia from Milan to Rome."

..."Finished on the 7th of July 1514 at 11pm in Belvedere – at the,work space "glorious" designed for my by "the Glorious". (quadrature of the circle)".

..."Ascension Day in Amboise, in Cloux, May 1517."

...About the year 1400 Rome with its 35,000 inhabitants was more of a village than a city. Through the stairs of the old Saint Peter's Cathedral grass was growing. The Pope made the decision to enlarge Rome as Their residence and began the reconstruction of Rome. Leonardo had been living in Rome for about 3 years at this time.

...In 1503 Pope Julius II decided to rebuild the Saint Peters Cathedral.

... The opening of the new cathedral was held in 1626, after 123 years of construction. They needed 40 years more to finish the interior decoration.

pic.26 Saint Peter's Cathedral in Rome

"...strange soul... ... which was always glancing at the infinity and the being behind."

Hippolyte Taine

...War was part of the everyday life in the Italian Renaissance, either against foreign invaders or internally within its own boundaries.

...Most of the city states were hiring foreign troups rather then sacrificing their own citizen in the endless wars.

...Machiavelli introduced later the concept of a popular army. Most of the soldiers came from the countryside.

...The older and richer families owned manors, where they lived for certain months every year.

...In the Tuscany were rows of groves of olives and vineyards next to each other. Fruits, nuts and grains were cultivated there as well.

... The leaseholders split the costs and the crops, when they had too much they sold the excess in the city.

MACHIAVELLI

...He was 14 years secretary of state, later he was banished to the "countryside", where he became a "political writer".

... His first work „Il principe - The prince" was "the first political theory of the modern times".

... Machiavelli lost the elections of the political appointee, who was responsible for the fortification of Florence.

...his rival candidate was Michel-angelo.

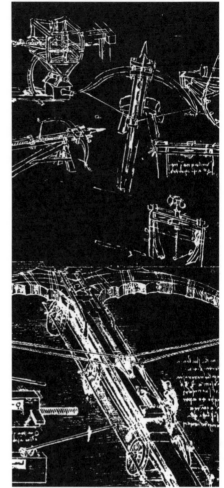

pic.27 warmachines by Leonardo

"Such a rare and universal person, that you could say, nature created him as a wonderment for itself"
unknown writer

pic. 28 nameless woman (Botticelli)

...**Sandro Botticelli**, an excellent painter, on wood panels as well as on walls" (Report from a artist-agent to Ludovico de Medici).

...Botticelli left Rome angry about the Pope, less because of his lack of taste and more because of he being behind with donations.

"On Wednesday the 9th of July in 1504 at 7 am died Ser Piero da Vinci, notary in the Palazzo della Podesta, my father. He was eighty years old. He left ten sons and two daughters."
Leonardo

...**Albrecht Dürer** used the dowry of his wife not for buying a house but to finance a trip to Venice: "Here I am a gentlemen, at home a cadger."

... „Obviously Dürer is missing models... ...he is working with boys, who have bad bodies, like that of most of the Germans" (Vasari is criticising nude drawing of Dürer).

Botticelli and Dürer

pic. 29 self-portrait by Albrecht Dürer

... Michelangelo was as well an archrival of Raffael. Even in his hour of death Michelangelo was convinced that everything what was good in the paintings of Raffael, he had learned from him.

... Michelangelo took the site management for the Saint Peter`s Cathedral from Raffael. He even let some of the works already done by Raffael to decompose.

... "To paint one beautiful woman, I have to see many beautiful women. Because of the want of beautiful women at the moment, I focus myself with an inner image (Raffael).

pic.30 David of Michelangelo

... In 1504 two murals were to be painted in the Palazzo Vecchio in Florence, one wall by Leonardo, the opposite wall by Michelangelo.

... The two paintings were never finished

... The two men had an extremely nervous relationship, which was visible during some meetings.

... „Painting is something for women." (Michelangelo)

... „Nothing more than a good stonemason, that is all that he is; my son, a good stonemason" (Father of Michelangelo).

Michelangelo and Raffael

Leonardo as an entertainer

... Leonardo immersed himself intensively in music. He played instruments, above all the Lyra. He gave classes, invented instruments and was fascinated with the phenomena of acoustics. As a singer he was held in high regard. He referred to music as the ephemeral figure of the unseen.

... At the court of Milan Leonardo was involved in the arrangement of weddings, receptions and processions. He designed settings for parties, costumes, masks and machines for the theater. He demonstrated legerdemains, invented special effects and picture puzzels. At the courts of the Sforzas he was often called "apparatore" or in French "arrangeur de fetes".

... Leonardo liked to write tales or stories. Stories like "The flea and the dog" or "The stone and the street" shed light on him as a man full of irony, who reflected a lot on the issue of human vainness, which ruled to world.

... „A painter was asked why the statutes he did of his children were so ugly while his paintings were so beautiful. He replied he does his painting by day and his children at night.

Amboise is located at the Loire, in one of the most beautiful districts of France. Leonardo lived in Amboise about three years till his death in 1519, following an invitation by the King of France François I.

pic. 31 Amboise

The Kings of France:

...Francois I. invited Leonardo without any conditions to France. He gave Leonardo beside board and salary the castle Cloux in Amboise as his residence.

Due to his enthusiasm Louis XII., antecessor of Francois I., wanted to remove "The last supper" from the wall and to bring it to France.

"For his contemporaries he seemed to possess an unsacred and secret wisdom... Leonardo affected his environment like someone who is listening to a, for other people, inaudible voice."

Walter Pater

Amboise

testament of Leonardo

„While I thought that I was learning how to live, I have been learning how to die."
Leonardo

pic.32 deathbed of Leonardo

pic.33 the castle in Cloux

...Leonardo dies in 1519 in the castle Cloux in Amboise in France.

The decedent:

… wishes for his funeral were comprised of sixty big wax candles, carried by sixty poor men, who were paid for their services...

...left to his butler Battista half of his garden, located outside of the city walls of Milan...

...left to his attendant Salai the other half of the same garden...

...left to his maidservant Maturina a coat out of nice black cloth …

…left F. Melzi, nobleman from Milan, all and any books, which are owned by the deceased at this time, as well as all instruments and paintings, which are related to his practice as a painter…

(summary of the testament of Leonardo, written the 23rd day of April in 1519, before Easter)

"It is a complaint of everybody that such a man should die, whose equal in creation is not in power of nature any more."
Francesco Melzi

"Not more from life he asked for than being useful."
Bernard Berenson

.."Lo and behold, man has a huge delusion, because he is continually working, just to be not in need, and thereby passes by his life hoping to enjoy once the goods, which he earned with his best effort."

.."The highest fortune becomes the main reason of misfortune and the peak of wisdom the reason of foolishness."

.."The water, which do you touch in rivers, is the last of that, what was, and the first of that, what will come. Also it is with the present time."

.."Every evil leaves sorrow in the memory, except the biggest evil, namely the death, which erases those memories together with the life."

.."As a well-spent day brings happy sleep, so life well used brings happy death."

.."Love is existing like light, which burns brighter, in the darker places it finds."

.."Love prevails over everything."

Leonardo philosophical

Leonardo the inventor

In addition to Leonardo`s interests in humanities, medicine, philosophy, natural sciences and arts he was mainly an inventor. In the capacity of an inventor he concentrated all his knowledge and all his experiences as a craftsman, as a scientist and as an artist into helping the people of his time, through all availible means. What he did that most of the time was determined by the demands and wishes of his clients mixed with his own intentions which were steeped in pragmatical reasoning. As it was he had to earn a living for himself as well as for his students and his footmen. For this reason he invented machines and apparatuses for warfare ashore and on the sea, construction machines to lift heavy weights, devices that moved in the air, into and under water and on earth, machines for the industrial as well as for agricultural use, measuring instruments, machine elements which were a basis for further inventions. He also created useless automatic machines, just to entertain his clients. Surprisingly many of Leonardo`s inventions are still in use today, 500 years later almost unaltered. You can point out for example the ball bearing, the worm gear, the bicycle or the parachute.

„Through the inventions of Leonardo physical strength was replaced by water, wind, steam and gunpowder. During the course of the years machines and machine elements became more and more the expression of his sympathy with the world."
B.Dibner

"When besieged by ambitious tyrants, I find a means of offence and defence in order to preserve the chief gift of nature, which is liberty."
Leonardo

War was in Italy part of the everyday life during the Renaissance, either against invaders or amongst each other. The vigor of an army indexed the political situation more and more. Because time demanded people who were capable of military prowess, people like Leonardo used his inventiveness to his advantange though under the auspices of the court of Ludovico Sforza in Milan. Leonardo tried to not just invent weapons, but also to improve the production, the shooting mechanism and the load cycle of existing weapon systems. He improved antique weapons like catapults, developed giant slingshots, an automatic crossbow construction, an armoured vehicle, cannons with breech-load and cooling, automatic cannons as a forerunner of the machinegun, burning bullets, poison-grenades and projectile filled with gunpowder. He turned special attention to the study and understanding of ballistics. In this he discovered through an empirical methodology that the flight path of projectiles is a physical phenomena, which lead to a much higher marksmanship of cannons. Leonardo also invented mechanisms, which made fortification impregnable. At the same time he invented systems to realize these fortifications. Folding scaling ladders, demountable bridges and platforms of piles and rolls were part of his contribution. The proposal to install guns on ships or the sketches of a submarine boat, which could "drill" other ships from the bottom attest in an impressive way to the visionary spirit of Leonardo in the field of warmachines.

war instruments

catapult machine

pic.34 general view of a catapult machine

The first approach of Leonardo towards the technics of war was the improvement and optimization of war instruments, which were known since the antiquity, like the catapult machine. His intensive analysis of these "antiquated" branches of military might have been due to the fact that firearms were still under development and were not performing in the manner desired and with reliability. In fact some of the improvements illustrate that improved sling machines had a higher rate of effectiveness than firearms. The throw machine transferred strain of force from the wooden level of the shaft using rope and cogwheel into the sling-movement.

"Some experiments with the model of the sling machine, which does not flag like the crossbow has lead me to notice how far the same counterweight throws different weights, but also to what extent you must alter the counter weight on the sling when you throw a constant weight."
Leonardo

"This is the vehicle (ship), which is protected against thunder-guns and it attacks other ships with thunder-guns. It is lined with sheet iron, because of the fire and in addition full with peaked nails, in order that enemies can not jump without prejudice onto it."

Leonardo

Boat with two hulls: Leonardo constructed different variations of aqueous warships to further combative effectiveness and possibilities within water, from armoured warships via a sickel-ship to a concrete design for a submarine boat. During the coarse of this exploration he also developed a boat with two hulls, respectively with a double skin, which protected the boat from sinking, in case of damage from the side by clips or rammers.

pic.35 Double-Hull-Boat

double-hull-boat

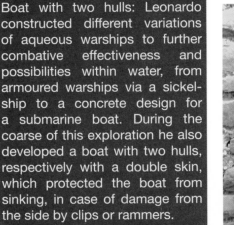

"This is a bridge, which has small wheels on it, or even better: a bridge, which rolls on small wheels, which stays on in one place.

Leonardo

pic.36 general view of a construction of bridge

pic.37 wheels

pic.38 Detail of construction

Mobile bridge and arched bridge: Leonardo built the easiest to construct and the most durable bridges, as exemplified in his application form to "Il Moro" to the court of Milan. This bridge could raise in a short time, was very stable and was constructed from easy to find and easily transportable materials (i.e tree trunks). The military mission was essential, the outcome of a battle often determined by the element of surprise as by unexpected crossing of rivers.

Within these constructions Leonardo utilized very effectively the strategic, basic rules, taking maximum advantage of the strength and durability of the materials.

bridges of Leonardo

pic.39 connection node

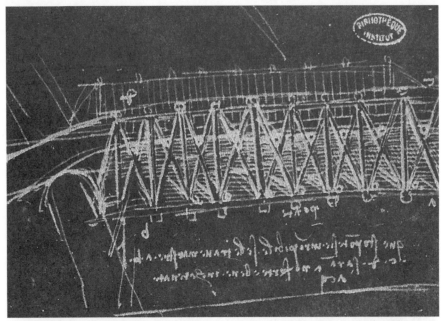

pic.40 sketch of a bridge

pic.42 arch bridge

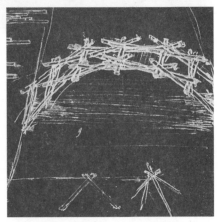

pic.41 Sketch of an arch bridge

tank

pic.43 general view of the tank

The success in moving, which other people envisioned happening with glidings, Leonardo realized through the use of a cogwheel construction located in the center of the tank, where upon the force of eight men was transferred via the central axis through crank-handles. In addition, Leonardo was also thinking about using horses instead of men, but the potential of loud noises causing agitation to them dissuaded him from this idea.

pic.44 construction detail

"...Eight men will shoot, and the same men will turn the cart and track the enemy. This vehiculuar is well used to break through the ranks, but it needs an attendant."

Leonardo

... The ballistic studies of Leonardo resulted in the increased marksmanship of projectiles. Through these experiments, one in which he was able to project a rocket 3,000 meters (app.9000feets) high, he discovered the role of air resistance. His experiments with projected water resulted in the idea that the shape of a projectile has to be that of a parabola. This lead him to the construction of lance-shaped projectiles which are still in use today, and allow for increased accuracy especially when aiming for long range targets. The projectiles were an optimised aerodynamic streamlined shape with a tail plane rudder.

Cognition of Leonardo:

"The air becomes denser in front of quickly moving bodies, in fact more or less dense depending upon whether the velocity is higher or less higher."

For short range targets Leonardo developed projectiles with an inner explosive force, which detonated in the air or a short time after impact into countless splitters, and is comparable to the „Dumdum" projectiles today.

pic.45 different types of projectiles

"This is the most mortal instrument, which exists. If the projectile in the middle impacts, it inflames the other ones on the side, and thereby the middle projectile burns and saunters the others, which catch fire before you can say Ave Maria."
Leonardo

pic.46 general view of the sickle-cart

pic.47 drive mechanism

pic.48 Detailed view

Sickle-carts had been used in acts of war already by the Romans. The cart was equipped with sickles, which were connected to a rotor causing them to turn where upon the vehicle moved. The rotation of the wheels was transfered mechanically into the rotor using cogwheels and shafts. The cart was pulled by horses, which often fell down within a short time due to hidden mantraps. This weapon also often reaped a higher amount of damage on friends then on enemies due to the fact that the horses often ran into their own ranks, startled by the acts of war around them.

„When this sickle-cart moves through your own ranks, you have to lift up the mechanism of the sickles, so that you didn't injure your fellow comrades."
Leonardo (tip for the own soldiers)

sickle-cart

... Leonardo's study of attack battleships was remarkable. The effectiveness of these weapons was based on rapidly moving up and down sickles, controlled by a crank handle and cogwheel-mechanism. The sickle was placed on a rotating platform, which when turned, moved downwards quickly to strike the target. A mast or a sail would have interfered with battleship efficiency. Substituting for sails were many oarsmen, who sat under the shelter of fresh hides, in order to protect them from lofted fires thrown by the enemy.

pic.49 detailed view of a sickle

pic.50 detailed view

pic.51 general view of the ship

"The counteragent results in giving the ships hawser out of chains in a height of six cubits."
Leonardo

battle ship with sickle

Leonardo tried to develop a battleship which in an unexpected fight at sea could be navigated by one man only. This man was also capable of handling the rectangular mortar which was placed on a rotating platform.

Huge gushes of fire are thrown by the mortar impact setting the hostile ships on fire and sinking them. Leonardo also suggested the use of poisoned missiles capable of choking the enemy.

pic. 52,53,54,55 gunboat in different positions

gunboat

pic.56 view from the inside,
front in action

..One of the various defence systems invented by Leonardo was this very simple system of repelling enemy ladders. If the enemies leaned their ladders against the wall being defended, they were overthrown by a bar which was set in motion by a hand gear.

pic.57 view from the outside,
not in action

pic.58 View from the outside, in action

„ And the operation to pull up such bares quickly has to be applied the way it is shown here."
Leonardo

„ He who is in league with the beginner, has to take a strong thread if he has to be on duty of the Kastellans. If the right time has come, the one having the thread has to lift a cable roll with which he again need to lift a wire, which then will be useful to raise the rope-ladder."

Leonardo (Instruction for secretly entering a fort)

pic.59 assaulting a fortress

pic.60 machine for assaulting a fortress

...Leonardo developed systems of defence as well as techniques for attacking. Here a man is shown, who, like an alpinist, punches his climbing irons into the wall of a fort, a technique which was very popular. Another method developed was to fix a rope-ladder at the battlement. This how ever required another person behind the battlement to assist.

pic. 61 detail of the tunnel

...Once one has reached close proximity to the wall, a bridge which looks like a housetop was fixed on the surface of the wall with the help of a cable winches, so that the invaders are able to break through this protective barrier.

assaulting a fortress

pic.62 defence of the enemy ladders

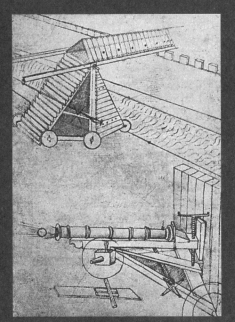

pic.63 assaulting a fortress

The dream of flying followed Leonardo all his life. His extensive studies of the birds' flight lead him through a number of years to the believe that man "simply" needed to follow the same mechanisms and movements used by birds. He wrote: "This is how you get proof from this listed evidence, that man is able to overcome the resisting air by putting pressure on it through his artistically added big wings which even allow him to fly up in the air." Only in his later years, he realized and accepted the fact that due to the anatomical misconception of man between weight and available power he would never be able to fly like a bird. Leonardo's aerial machines which he developed later already followed the principles of gliding flights, using wind and streaming.

Leonardo's suggestions in case of a crash:

"Bags by which a man falling from a height of 6 braccia may avoid hurting himself, by a fall whether into water or on the ground; and these bags, strung together like a rosary, are to be fixed on one's back. If you fall with a double hose the one you wear underneath your buttocks, so make sure, that you have it when you hit the ground."
"You need to test this device above a lake and wear a long hose as a belt, to avoid drowning upon crashing."
Leonardo

Airborne transportation

„ A cable arches the wing, one is turning it with the help of a hand gear, a third is dropping it down, a fourth is carrying it from the bottom to the top......Under the body between the groove of the cervix and the breastbone should lay a chamois leather."

Leonardo's operating instruction

pic.65 detail

...This illustrates a bird-flying machine where a man pedals in a sloped position with the help of cable winches and hand gears which facilitate up lifting and dragging under as well as driving the wings. This is comparable to a rear tail wing rudder of airplanes today. The feet fit in a kind of stirrup where one foot lifts one of the wings up while the other one gets lowered. Leonardo gave precise instructions for the position of the pilot, determining exactly where the heart of the pilot should lay on the base of the machine. This mechanism was meant to be a „wing-bicycle" manageable in a horizontal position.

pic.66 view of the „wing-bicycle"

bird wing machine

What weight can a wing have? With this invention Leonardo tried to prove the most practicable wing size, which a human being is still able to move. According to his studies the wing has to be 12 meters long and wide.

pic. 67 for the exhibition the wing was fixed. (normally it was moveable)

„If you want to prove the wing properly, then one should use a cardboard which is hardened through a net. Then form the main bar using reed and give the wing at least a length and wideness of 20 cubits and fix it on a bar having a weight of 200 pounds. Then operate strongly as it is shown above."

Leonardo

flap-wing

" If this helical machine is well done, namely of canvas whose pores are sealed up with strong paste and when it gets turned around quickly then, this screw will escalate and rise."

Leonardo

pic.69 sketch „Airscrew"

...This machine is probably one of Leonardo's most well known designs as one can see the very beginnings of a modern helicopter in it. It is comprised of a flying screw which centers a vertical axis. The screw has a radius of 4.8 meters (app. 15 feets) and is strung with linen, it's border being composed of metal wire.

The airscrew works with the help of a crank gear which unwinds the wire being rotated around a central axis by humans.

Leonardo thought that the screw by means of heavy torque became as he said a „nut" causing the machine to eventually soar.

pic.68 „Airscrew"

„Airscrew"

...This project again shows how excellent and progressive Leonardo's ideas were. The extremely precise instructions on how to build this parachute are exceptional given that at that time, 500 years ago, no one knew anything about flying except for birds. This parachute, an original copy, was tested by athletes five years ago and has been proven to be a working prototype!

pic.70 parachute

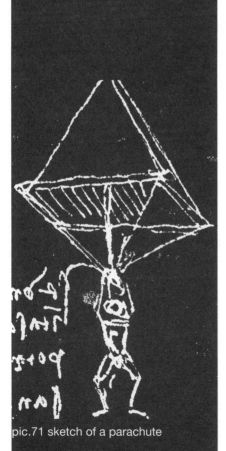

pic.71 sketch of a parachute

„ If a human being has got a tent roof over his head which is of sealed canvas and has got a wide and length of 12 ells, he is able to fall from very high without suffering any harm."

Leonardo

pic.72 gliders

...The material used was bamboo and canvas for the connecting piece, the cable winch being comprised of floss and leather. Under the wings, which have a span of 10 meters, is the hanger where the pilot is positioned.

While flying, this hanger carries the pilot in a vertical position differing from modern constructions.

The wings are built similar to wings of big birds the outer section being navigated by the pilot using cords. From watching birds closely Leonardo deduced that the inner section of the wings needed to move slower than the outer sections. The outer section also had to be supported by the inner one.

pic.73 head section

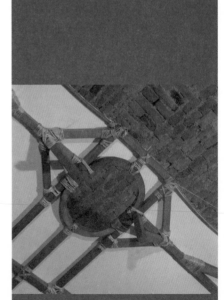

pic.74 head-passage detailed

glider

pic.75 position of the pilot

pic.77 head support with
arm support

„ Vorticity of air in case of birds is getting absorbed near the appendage of the wings. The fourth law of weight says: The part of the bearer which is closer to the base, is the stronger one."
Leonardo

pic. 76 flying apparatus

flying apparatus

pic.78 general view of the hang glider

... Leonardo's pursuit of flying machines can be divided into two periods. The very first flying machines were fueled by means of human power. Because he realized that human power wasn't sufficient he started using wind and vector energy. This hang glider is one of these types of flying machines, its flight path navigated through the use of a rudder. Leonardo never created fixed wings as are common today.

„Supposed a body would glide in the air here like a bird which cranks his tale in different declinations, you will derive a general rule of different cambers of birds movement using the bending of the tale."

Leonardo

pic. 79 attachment of the pilot

hang glider

„Tomorrow let some different formed bodies of card board glide in the air leaving from our gangway and then draw the figures and movements each one performs while sliding down."

Leonardo (concerning on trials with flying models)

...After closely studying a bird's anatomy, Leonardo incorporated observations made from these studies into his flying models. First he explored the idea of divided wings, followed by a single wing, which is similar to a bat's wing. The wing consisted of wooden and bamboo bars and was covered with a natural fiber cloth.
There was a crank rolling a cable winch on a spool. The pilot sat on a gondola.

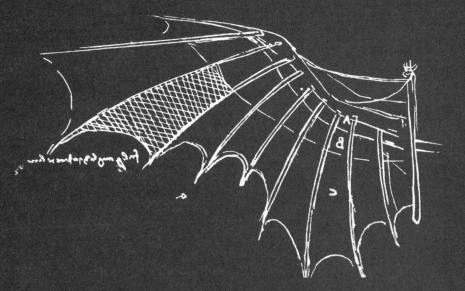

pic.80 study of a wing

study - wing formation

pic.81 bird wing apparatus

pic.82 insight into the gondola

...Here a man standing upright activates the engine of the flying machine using his head and hands which are embedded into something like a gondola. Leonardo publishes the measurements: Ladder for boarding 12 ells high, wing span 40 ells, body of the gondola 20 ells cross section dimension and 5 ells high. Considering the dimension Leonardo regards it as necessary to install two pairs of wings which intersect.

bird wing apparatus

„The movement of the wings runs like the trot of a horse. On this account I argue that this machine is better than any other."
Leonardo

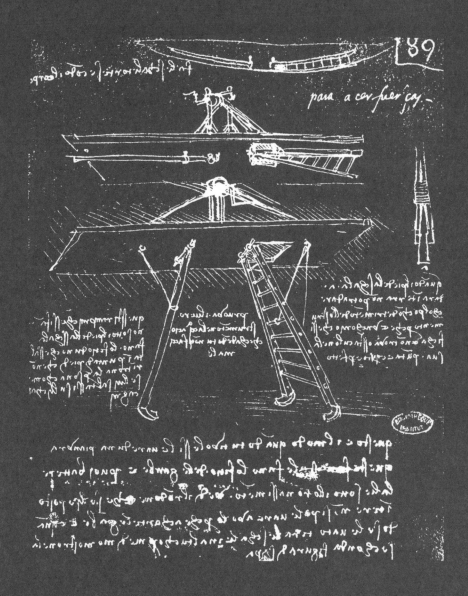

pic.83 flying machine with ladder

Leonardo not only dealt with different forms of actuation concerning ships, as for example the paddle drive, but was also deeply engaged in finding the best shape for the hull. His studies proved that the hull shape is very important for reaching faster speeds as determined by length, amplitude and the depth of the ships body. For this purpose he concerned himself with the anatomy of fish using it as an example to construct nonresistant keels. Further he tried to develop under water vehicles which are comparable with today's submarines. His diving suits were already equipped with two outlets, an intake for oxygen and an outlet for nitrogen. Swimming-gloves, similar to present day flippers, and a rescue- tire filled with air are by all means comparable to modern resolutions.

movement on water

pic.85 paddle-wheel boat

…With his nautical inventions, Leonardo strove for flexibility and effectiveness. In doing so the form of the ship was very important and played a large role in how one was geared to the form, which determined the degree of revving power and speed, similar to the mechanics of a fish. He set up ships with paddle wheels which were activated by means of a crank and were feet- or hand- operated. A sweep wheel was added to increase the efficiency.

pic.86 actuation detail

pic.87 drawing of a mechanical shovel excavator

boat with paddle wheel

...Useful for cleaning and servicing of canals and port basins. Leonardo created an excavator installed on top of two ships having four shovels which were set in rotation by a hand gear. With this technique the mud could be removed from the ground. The mud fell in a third boat which was placed between the other two boats. The wheel rotated a cord which was fixed at the shore and was coiled up around the axis of a barrel, whereby the barrel was moved to other sides of the ship, distributing the mud across both sides. The barrel could also be moved in a vertical position in order to regulate the depth of the distribution.

pic. 89 mechanical shovel excavator

pic.88 Detail

„But reader, you should realize that this has a use which will appear in the economy of time. This saving derives from the fact that the machine, which lifts the earth from the bottom to the top, constantly performs this promotion activity and never reverses again."
Leonardo commenting on the effectiveness of the mechanical shovel

mechanical shovel excavator

pic.90 Water-ski Detail

pic.91 water-ski

pic.92 sketch

...Leonardo didn't invent methods of moving across water by means of swimming-shoes and swimming-sticks, and in fact presented them as already made objects as he had done with swimming-gloves as well. The fact that he was incredibly interested in the mechanics of these sorts of objects is proof that he had investigated principles of the locomotion of man on water. It is how ever unknown who originally invented this swimming device.

water-ski

...Among Leonardo's inventions concerning the issue of „aquatic movement" was, besides a diving apparatus', water-skis and swimming gloves and a drawing of an oxygen belt. He suggested this technique in order to avoid being drowned in case of windstorm and shipwreck at sea. They used leather so that the oxygen belt was water proved. The volume can be changed by means of air injection whereas the air inside the belt functions not only as an ascending force in case of emergency, but also as a device for respiration which was provided by an additional tube.

...The idea of an underwater breathing apparatus was not new and was already used when diving for pearls in the Indian ocean. The tube was strengthened through rings so that it was resistant against unevenly distributed pressure. Leonardo's concept was distinguished from the others due to the manner and variety details which improved already existing breathing apparatus', which were always anticipating keeping modern solutions. An example would be the outlet for the inflow and outflow of air.

pic.93 diving-mask

pic.94 floating tire

pic.95 sketch

„ One need to have a robe made of leather which has double borders of finger breadth on the bosom and should be duplicated from the belt to the knee. If you must jump into the sea, then blow up the laps of your robe, jump into the sea and be driven by the waves....

Leonardo's instructions for the floating tire

The aim of the military division was most likely to create vehicles, which could move independently and with ease in front of horses, who were susceptible to injury. This contrasted with civilian life which at that time was not in noticeable demand of vehicles that ran independent of harnessed animals.

Nevertheless Leonardo developed rather incidentally as a by-product, different mechanical inventions for civilian use. The modern car and the modern bicycle are examples of inventions within history that arose out of other incidental inventions. As we learn from the quotations below he also studied the smallest details of human movement patterns, aiming for new ideas that might emerge out of these rigorous observations.

„Anyone going downhill is using short steps because the weight rests on the back of one's feet, anyone going uphill is using long steps because the weight rests on the front of one's feet"
Leonardo commenting on pace

"A definition as to tell me why a man who slides on ice does not fall."
Leonardo observing a man sliding on ice.

movement on land

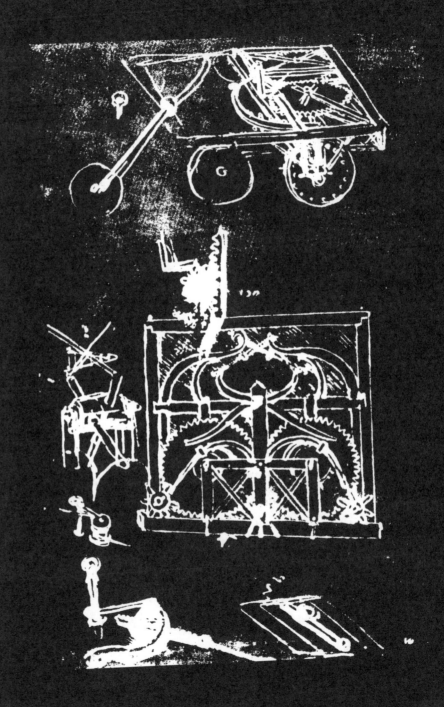

pic.96 view of the automobile

The back wheels of the self moving vehicle are equipped with a differential gear that can be moved from the front wheal independently. A fourth wheel is connected with a kind of rudder which helps to drive the car. The actuation is produced through a complicated crossbow-clip mechanism, and through means of relaxation of several clips transmits the power to the wheels- similar to a toy car with spring-type connections. One should be aware of the great effort placed on the driver who constantly has to bend the clips while driving. „This is an early prototype of the first car in the world" presumably devised for courtly activities.

pic.97 crank for „drawing on"

pic.98 actuation transmittance

pic.99 actuation with clips

„But when you displace the two back wheels with higher ones the car will move more easily then….the movement is so much harder the lower the smaller one is in comparison to the first one."

Leonardo commenting on the movement of a car

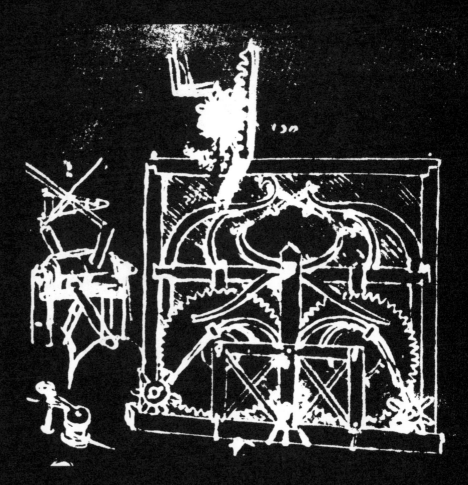

pic.100 drawing of the automobile

pic.101 „bicycle"

pic.102 detail of bicycle chain

In the „Codex Atlanticus" there is an illustration of a bicycle. Because of the clumsy and inexplicit design of the drawing and based on Leonardo's signature, it was already expected that this was not a work of Leonardo himself. Solari possibly saw the drawing in Leonardo's studio and made a copy of it. It is equipped with foot pedals, a chain drive and a handlebar. The bicycle is made of wood. This drawing was discovered around 50 years ago between the stuck together sheets of the Codex Atlanticus. The possibility of a falsification has been argued against as this bicycle does not resemble any models which were invented later, and due to the fact that they use a chain drive with angular elements which were not considered for use with a bicycle at the time, and without any doubt came from Leonardo.

Upper Bavarian Government, Munich   Guest House, Federal Rep. of Germany   Jewish Museum, Berlin (Daniel Libeskind)

We develope and produce varnish, oil, wax and maintenance products for surface protection of wood, parquet, cork....

IRSA

IRSA Lackfabrik
Irmgard Sallinger GmbH
D-86489 Deisenhausen
Germany
Tel: 0049-8282-8944-0
Fax: 0049-8282-8944-44

email: info@irsa.de

www.irsa.de

Leonardo's machines on the one hand served for improving the situation of the working population on land, and on the other hand helped to optimize and rationalize urban operating processes. Above all these machines were concerned with lifting and moving heavy items with the help of cranes such as wood forms, the handling and fabrication of metals, the transportation of water and machines for handling thread and cloth, as well as machine tools.

„In order to drill through a bar it (the bar) has be to upright and should be drilled from the bottom, so that the hole deflates itself…
Leonardo commenting on the power drill

mechanical tools

This saw mill is activated by water power. The rotary motion of the water wheel is transformed into a stroke movement whereby the vertical installed saw blade moves up and down. In principle this saw mill is a semi-automated installation.

pic.103 detail of the saw mill

pic.104 general view of the hydraulic saw

pic.105 detail

pic.106 detail

pic.107 detail

pic.108 vertical drilling machine

The apparatus operates from the bottom to the top by means of a screw which is activated by men. Between the earth's surface and the screw there is a kind of hopper which is supposed to prevent the earth from falling upon the worker's head.

„Why is the little drill engine doing this hole without a direction? And why does the big one need to be turned twice or third times if this hole should be expanded?"

Leonardo about the problem of drills in different sizes

pic.109 excavation engine

The tub of this graver works through rapid disengagement of the weight utilizing its dormant kinetic energy. The big semi-flywheel lifts the excavation tub and drops the weight. This process recurs until the tub on the bottom digs into the culvert. Then the graver gets hauled to a new digging.

This apparatus, used for setting up pillars, was improved and perfected by Leonardo only in details, but not invented by him. A gear sets in motion a rolling stand on which the pillar lays. The pillar gets lifted with a helical gear, which is fixed at the opposite end of the pillar. In order to facilitate turning the crank the nut is placed on a roller bearing.

…This construction deals with an automated, variable clamp grip. The more load this gripper bears the more power with which the load is held.

pic.110 general view

pic.111 detail of the die set

pic.112 safety tonge

pic.113 automated clamp

pic.114 crane with central jack

pic. 115 rotary crane

...Leonardo invented an automated hook with counterweight where the load detaches automatically from the clamp connection once the load is redistributed on the ground.

The power restraining the counterweight drops out and spins down and is counterbalance through the weight. The clamp in this context moves up and slips out of the hanger.

pic. 117 drawing of a crane

pic.118 circular plate/disk crane

Florence at that time was virtually an open air building lot. When Brunelleschi had completed the cupola of the cathedral and Verrocchio's workshop was given the commission to fix a cuprous globe on top, Brunelleschi's hoist engines were faced with a new challenge. Many engineers were actively working on improving the functional capacities of cranes and elevators. Leonardo, too, made several contributions and developed these special cranes having a bearing gear with central jacks, especially in regards to the building of a round cupola.

pic.119 view through the hole in the wall

pic.120 mirror room

…The field of optics was also a part of Leonardo's interests. The walls were lined with mirrors. Leonardo used this reflection-room for his drawings and paintings. Through a whole in the wall one can see the model from all sides simultaneously.

It was Leonardo's ambition to understand the laws of nature in order to be able to utilize their powers and effects. He studied reasons behind the different states in natural phenomena such as the formation of clouds, wind, steams, humidity and tides. There was also an exploration into what determined distances, heights and the weight of these different types of phenomena. He invented measuring apparatuses which enabled him to observe and index different states of these phenomena, an example being an instrument for measuring air moisture, wind force, wind pace, and distance.

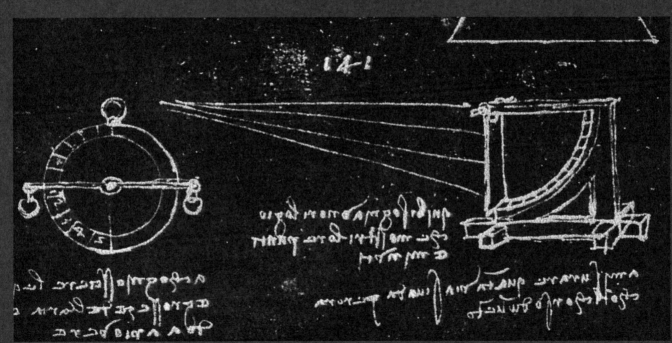

pic.121 drawing of the measuring instruments

pic.122 plate wind measuring instrument

Leonardo was not only involved with the planning and building of flying machines, but also with flying control instruments such as this wind gauge. This apparatus was also used to measure distance covered at sea through wind calculations. In this model the slew able bedded small plate moves up in correlation to the amount of force the wind applied. The notches underneath the small plate serve as a display.

„For this, one needs a clock which shows the hours, minutes and seconds in order to measure how far one can get with the help of wind flow within one hour."
Leonardo

This device enabled the measurement of the power of air resistance. This anemometer consists of two canonical formed channels having variable cross-section-dimension and a blower-like a wheel with a counterweight. With this one can prove if the wind, which sets the wheel in motion, is acting commensurate to the hole of the channels where the air passes through.
The wind power is the same for both holes. It is a commonly held belief that Leonardo was the first to measure wind flow in this sophisticated type of manner.

pic.123 anemometer

This apparatus consists of a pendulum and a clock, which aids in the navigation through wind. The inclinometer helps to orientate the flying machine horizontally through measuring pitch. In principle this kind of inclinometer is still in use at today's airplanes.

„…in order to drive the flying apparatus, in a straight or sloping position, as you want, that means: if you want to go straight make sure the ball is standing in the middle of the circle."

Leonardo

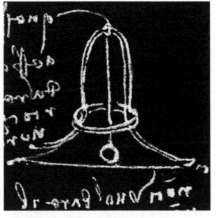

pic.124 sketch

pic.125 inclinometer

For Leonardo, the discipline of mechanics was comprised of mathematic cognitions which were transferred into the practical applications as an integral part of the reasoning behind one's argument. He thought of mechanics as the paradise of the mathematic science, because through this one could reach mathematic progeny. It was considered an art from which various assortments of machines, instruments, technical devices and others like were constructed. Leonardo illustrated a broad knowledge of simple machines that had been in existence since the times of the ancient world. On this basis he developed a unique creativity and quality when it came to building machines and elements.

He persisted, direct as well as indirect, path breaking up to the present in many technical fields. In this regard he invented and improved „building blocks" as recurrent standardized elements, which were integral in the operation and construction of bigger, often more complicated machines.

This included: ball bearings, clutches, keys, rivets, cords, chains, gear wheels, outlets, tappets, tackles, fly wheels, gears, movement-transformers, spring tension as well as many others. Leonardo used the „screw" in a very unique manner that differed from its popular application at the time. Starting with the mechanism of a watch he developed many different types of movement transformation and as well as new ways of utilizing spring tension.

mechanics

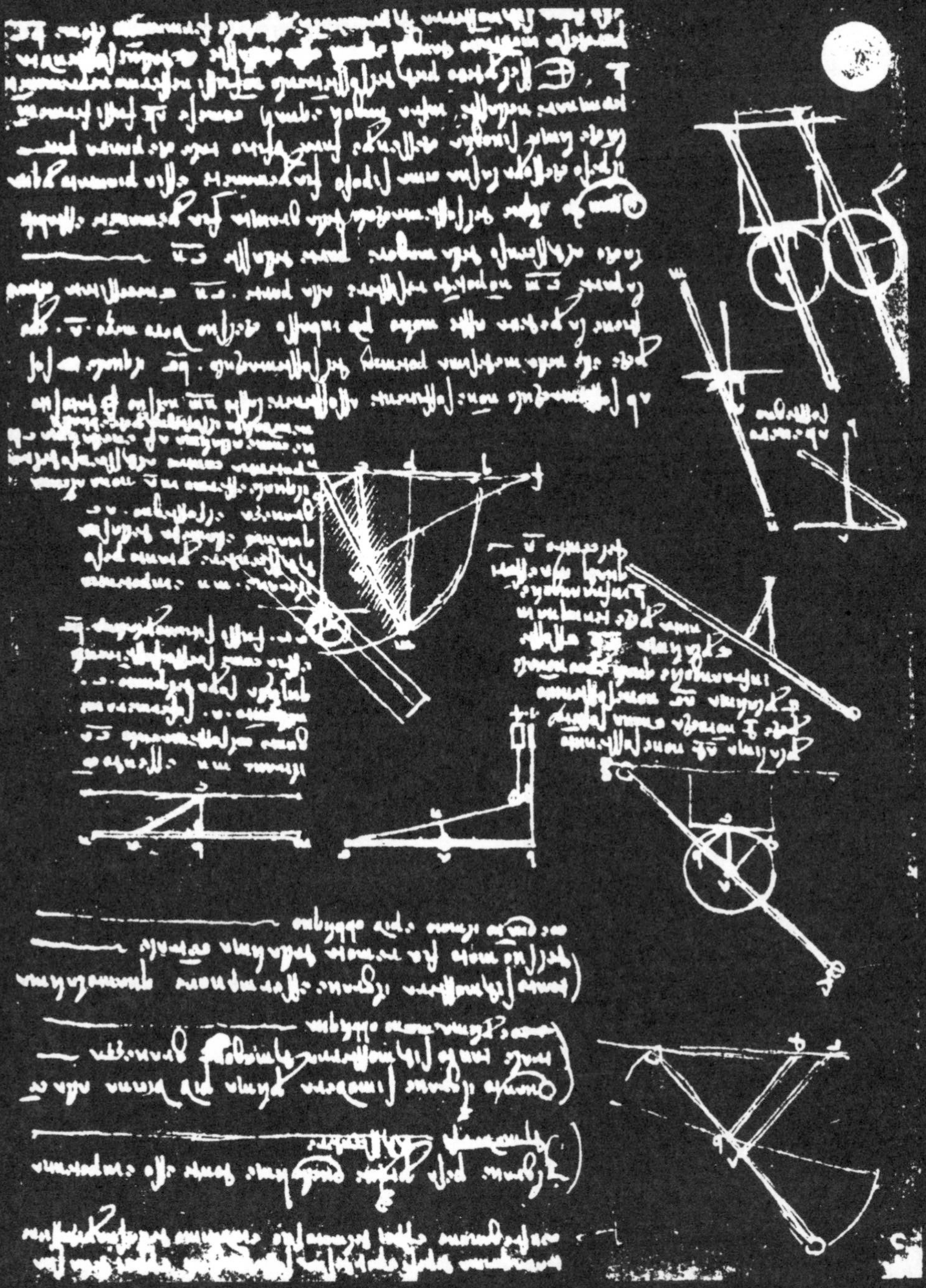

pic.126 drawing of the mechanic

This gear by Leonardo was especially integral to the movement of vehicles. The movement of the wheal was transferred from one level to another via this gear. If movement starts on the vertical level it transfers the movement to the horizontal level. Leonardo, in particular had analyzed the resistance, capacity and threshold of these different items.

„...The teeth wear off twice as much because they have to stand two movements.

Leonardo commenting on the combination gear wheel-lantern wheel

pic.127 cog wheel

Leonardo made several improvements to the Archimedes screw. This consisted of a helical tube, which was rotated around a barrel. The water is pushed into the tube via the rotation where upon the conveyance screw lifts it up. Leonardo's version creates less friction and seeping through the delivery of a constant flow of water.

pic.128 Archimedes screw

pic.129 detail above

pic.130 detail bottom

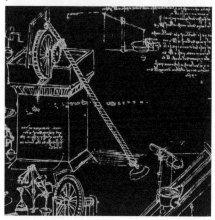

pic.131 sketch

„With the principle of lifting any river can be led over a high mountain."
Leonardo

Archimedes screw

chain drive

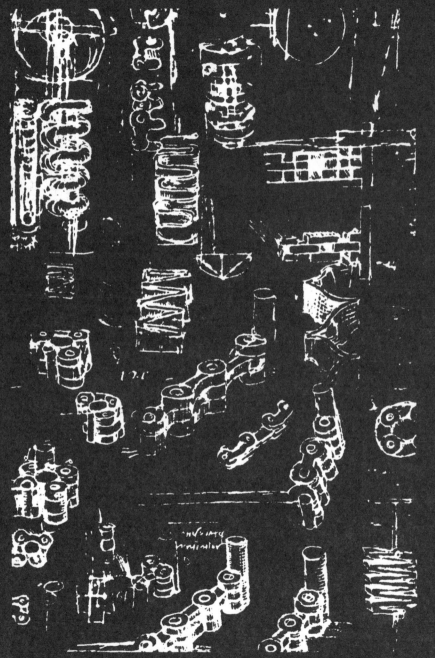

...Leonardo studied many different types of flexible chain drives in order to achieve continuous movement. The cogging of the wheel, having a shape of dice, and the attached weights illustrate that this chain wasn't designed for continuous movements as is for example found in watches. Leonardo used this chain drive in one of his most famous machines the bicycle. But what he didn't know at that time was that the angular teeth would make a continuous drive impossible. Later he fixed this problem through rounded chain elements which are still in use today.

pic.132 drawing of the chain drive

pic.133 chain drive

...To find methods for lifting heavy weighted objects was one of the most pressing goals of engineers at that time.
Leonardo drew many studies of an apparatus that dealt with this problem. The apparatus consisted of a crank, a reduction transformer of two gear wheels and one ridged pole, which could be wound up and down. The mode of operation is identical with how one would change a car wheel.

pic.134 drawing car-jack

pic.135 car-jack

car-jack

pic.136 screwing gear wheel

pic.137 detail

… The „screw" played an important role in Leonardo's mechanical inventions. He developed many types of application for the screw and implemented it into his designs in numerous ways.

This drive was developed by Leonardo and was a combination of an endless screw with a gear wheel. There was a big advantage in the amount of power transferred, allowing it to operate safely and durably, with low strains and requiring a low rotational speed. This drive is well known as a snake drive and is widely in use within the field of engineering still today.

„If you deal with heavy weights do not get involved with ferric teeth because one teeth could easily break, in this case take the screw....but this should be used for pulling and not for pushing."

Leonardo

...Leonardo was very interested in finding techniques for reducing friction. Here 8 concave barrels, which can rotate freely, are prevented from touching the balls. The ball- and barrel-system clearly reduces friction. This is also due to the fact that the surface lying on top can turn faster and easier despite heavy loads that were to be carried. Indeed barrels and bearings have been used since the ancient world, but not the ball-bearing with non-touching surfaces as was developed by Leonardo. This principle is still used today in almost all applications that utilize ball-bearings.

pic.138 ball-bearing with barrels

pic.139 ball-bearing without barrels

„Balls and rolls, if they touch each other while moving, complicate the movement more than without touching each other."

Leonardo

„When doubling the weight the friction gets effective twice."

Leonardo commenting on the basic principle of friction power

pic.140 bll-bearing with spindle

pic.141 detail

...Leonardo worked, in connection with the transformation of movement, on different means to minimize the problem of friction. In order to face, for example, the pressure of a vertically mounted axis he suggested a bearing where the vertical load would be diverted via balls and skittles.

„Three balls positioned under the spindle are better than four because the three of them are for sure always touched by the spindle and are moved regularly. With four there is a danger that one of them stays untouched."
Leonardo

ball-bearing with spindle

A flying wheel consists of a real wheel plus weights hung on a chain. The weights add additional stored kinetic energy in terms of rotary motion and help to overcome moments of inertia as well as to lessen the amount of power required to drive the wheel. The oscillating weights are hung in such way that movement is unimpeded. The principle of oscillating weights has been used over time for many different types of machinery, as both a means to balance and to store energy.

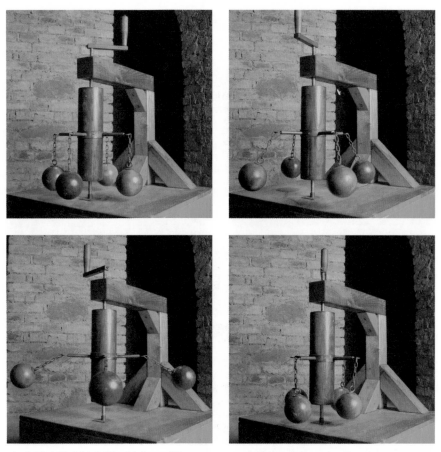

pic.142,143,144,145 studies of the movement of the flying wheel

„It is then reported on the retched wheel and its plug, on the flying wheel, on cords, tackles, winches and barrels."
Leonardo

pic.146 pulley

This study demonstrates the lifting of heavy objects with little effort. The weight is arranged regularly on all rolls and reduces the amount of energy exerted. The enormous amount of friction is avoided here. Leonardo dealt with the problem of lifting of weights through the combination of several loose rolls and cords. This led to the understanding of the interplay between elements where upon one could calculate in advance how the elements fit together with the utmost precision. In this context Leonardo is given credit for this work.

„The cord doubles its natural strength as often as it is put up in different work pieces of its length."

Leonardo

...This eccentric hammer is for an engine, which was driven mainly by water power and was used as a forging tool. The tappet, which was placed on the camshaft in turn created a stroke like movement, generating the up and down motion of the hammer.

pic.147 camshaft

pic.148 eccentric hammer

„I argue that the anvil cannot sound because it is not suspended ....however because you hear different sounds under hammers of different sizes the sound is in the hammer and not in the anvil."

Leonardo (concerning the question where the sound comes from)

eccentric hammer

pic.149 detail of connecting rod

...Leonardo's engines work through tranformation principles of movement. The connecting rod is a mechanical element between two parts of an engine, which are transformed in an alternating linear movement and through a continuous circular motion.

...This kind of transformation movement is used in all motor driven vehicles.

pic.150 connecting rod

... The illustration shows the transformation of movement on the axis of a carriage. The winder pushes a journal wheel which causes the rotation of the lantern cogwheel. The movement is converted onto only one wheel, which allows the second wheel to rotate at a different speed.

pic.151 differential

pic.152 detail

pic.153 sketch

pic.154 gear shift

… These types of gears are used to change the speed of various processes. The illustration shows a conical wheel which influences cogwheels of different diameters. Each of those has a different speed and consequently different rates of rotation. Today, these gear systems are applied in all vehicles that use gears.

... In addition, Leonardo was very intensively focused on all perpetual movement, a theme widely discussed by intellectuals.

... Leonardo very carefully analyzed several ideas of how the perpetuum work and used a balanced wheel with unfixed weights to eventually prove that perpetual movement was impossible.

... The centre of a weight that is meant to set the wheel in motion will always lie underneath the turning point of the wheel.

pic.155 Leonardo´s proof of the impossibility of the Perpetuum Mobile

"Oh, you explorers of perpetual movement, how many idle fantasies have you created during your quest! You had better joined the gold-hunters!"
Leonardo

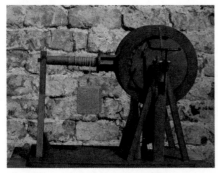

pic.156 model of transformation

pic.157 detail

pic.158 detail

Here we have the transformation of an inconsistent movement into a constant one with a machine used to lift weights, a process in which an alternating movement is converted into a continuous movement (i.e. from an oscillating to constant movement). The handle on the right of the machine is moved forwards and backwards, which starts the locking process of the cogwheel. This then moves a gear similar to a lantern, which is connected to a shaft in order to lift the weight attached.

"Each force that creates movement exerts more pressure on the exact point where it pushes itself off than on the object this force actually moves."
Leonardo

.... The use of this mechanism was particularly valid for machines that had to lift heavy weights. It consists of a cogwheel with acute-angled cogs and a blunt hook that grips each of the cogwheel's individual cogs. This way the wheel cannot turn in the opposite direction.

pic.159 autolock mechanism

pic.160 detail

"In case you are using a screw that grips only one cog of the wheel, it is necessary that you equip it with a closing pawl, so that the wheel doesn't turn backwards should the cog break....... otherwise it would cause great damage and destruction."

Leonardo

autolock mechanism

pic.161 detail

pic.162 detailed „inner-life"

pic.163 „robot"

... Leonardo had invented various devices with automated mechanisms of movement, which were based on his earlier inventions, such as the clock mechanisms. He used them for theatre purposes or other festivities, for example the large automated lion which he built for King Francois I. This lion would approach the king where upon his chest box would open, revealing white lilies. Another example is the "robot-soldier", who automatically saluted when the King walked past him.

Leonardo the genius

Everybody knows Leonardo da Vinci?

Everyone does, of course. He is the old man who is world-famous for creating the "Mona Lisa"! If Leonardo da Vinci was still alive today, many of us would still be surprised by his genius! At parties and festivals he would probably stand behind the stage, looking tall, strong, toned and very charming, wearing a short coat, generally well-groomed with his long, slightly curled hair. His job would be the one of the "apparatore", today known as „event manager". He was responsible for the smooth operation of the program- and would have been involved in the planning, 500 years ago, of events at the "court" of Milan or Florence. Leonardo himself would also most likely have performed using his own invention, the lyra, singing along to it between the festive speeches and greetings of the honourable guests. And he might even have asked of the audience to solve a riddle. He would have arranged a rather modest and light buffet: It would have consisted of bread, eggs, vegetables and mushrooms, because he was also a vegetarian. And wine, too, would be rare, for according to him, wine takes revenge on its drinkers! What was even more impressive were ose events he created that utilized special effects, cinematic elements, costumes and masks! Matching stage techniques left the audience in amazement. Near the entrance, for example, he would have positioned one of his inventions, the automated robot-soldiers, which would by design salute when those in charge (today's equivalent of politicians) walked past. Or he would have used pyrotechnics to create breath-taking fireworks.
Could you have imagined that Leonardo was occupied with such rather trivial and superficial engagements? He who is famous for the most well-known pieces, Madonna in the cave "Mona Lisa", "The Last Supper", etc.

Let us look at a quotation worth mentioning- by Berenson, the art historian:

'Painting meant so little to Leonardo that it can only be regarded as a means of the genius expression which he chose whenever he had no other important business to mind …"

And, Leonardo very often had more important business to mind, as only about a dozen of his paintings are finished, but those amongst them are the most famous ones in the world. What was it that kept Leonardo so busy that he could not spare time for painting? His interest in the human body, for instance.

Leonardo da Vinci was back then, about 500 years ago, probably the world's foremost scholar on anatomy: he meticulously dissected around 40 corpses, recording in detail extensive notes and drawings. He concentrated on physiology, always questioning things such as: "What creates the tone of a voice? What does the human being consist of? How do children grow in their mother's womb? What causes death?" His view of doctors at the time was critical, as the medical methods back then tended to do more harm than good.

Additionally, Leonardo was an architect who planned cities. For him it was an important issue to plan the "ideal city". Today's Pentagon is based on principles Leonardo invented, similar to the "city on different levels", a concept he came up with to solve problems regarding urban life.

Leonardo was very intensively focused on arming techniques, as well. On the one hand his interests were pragmatically driven, while on the other hand he was very patriotic. As a result, he focused on the techniques of war, including everything from tanks to "chemical" weapons which he had exclaimed could explode so quickly one wouldn't even be able to utter the words "Ave Maria". Constructing machine-tools and agricultural equipment, he tried to make labour easier for society's working class, for instance: lifting weights with cranes, the oil press, a water-driven sawmill, machines to wind ropes, devices for spinning, drills, production of files, grinding machines for mirrors etc.

Leonardo the genius

Leonardo the genius

The issue of machinery elements was important to him, for example: ball bearing, chair drive, gears, transformers for movements etc. An innumerable amount of today's machine parts have their origin in Leonardo's work. He also invented vehicles like the bicycle and the first individually moving means of transportation, today known as a car, which preceded the inventions that would take place a few centuries later. The matter of flying was one of his main areas of interest. Here, The so-called "bird's flight" and building "flying objects" formed the centre of his attention. The most famous examples are both the helicopter (air screw) and the parachute. Given that, Leonardo's knowledge is what Etrich and Lilienthal based their work on. Other fields arousing his interest were mathematics and geometry. Leonardo's specific focal point here was the problem of area-transformations and the "quadrature of the circle" which he had managed, according to his own account, on July 7th, 1514, at 11 p.m. He dealt with hydraulics and water construction such as building water roads and lock systems as those, which are still presently used. Moreover, he dealt with optics and astronomy, with the refraction of light to answer questions such as, "Why is the sky blue?" He applied lenses and telescopes even before Galilei, considered the moon which he suspected to have lakes. It was already a few years before Kopernikus that Leonardo sensed there had to be a heliocentric world system, for he wrote: "The sun does not move!" Another occupation of his was in the area of mechanics and the problem of gravity, a phenomenon which he discovered long before Newton. He was also interested in the movement on and through water. His inventions in this field are amongst others: the snorkel, the underwater boat, an air-filled life belt and the double-walled ship hull. Generally speaking, in spite of all his genius ideas, Leonardo considered "nature itself" to be the true and constantly available source of knowledge. All of Leonardo's findings are based on observing nature and experimenting with it. This probably made him the first person who systematically dealt with the combined topic of bionics. It seems impossible to grasp the extent of Leonardo's genius, but scientists, writers, philosophers, historians and even kings of several generations have tried. Here are some examples:

„The more you deal with Leonardo's work, the less you understand how a single person got that far, contributing so much in so many fields."
E. Gombrich

"He could never have believed that someone else in the world would have known as much as Leonardo. Not merely as a sculpturer, painter or architect, but also as a philosopher."
King Francois I.

„He resembled someone who had woken up too early in the darkness while the others were still sleeping."
D. Merezkovsky

Leonardo the genius

Anatomists have existed since the ancient world. The most well known among them was Galen, a Roman academic. What didn't exist were anatomical drawings. Leonardo built upon this base and produced drawings in a unique quality, in content as well as in graphical elaboration. In part he used a display format, which unified multiple perspectives in one drawing. Of these conclusions he was the first to discover them.

…"I confess to the people the origin of the second - no, the first or maybe also the second reason of their being."

…"You will give rule and dimension to each muscle and explain all their functions and how they are used and whatmoves them."

…"The wind in the bowel is created by the needless stuff, which accumulates in the rectum. It (the needless stuff) dries and causes severe pains, when it is enclosed in the colon."

…"I want to slice the liver till that point, where it masks the stomach, and see, how the veins branch out in the liver."

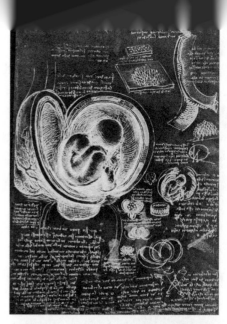

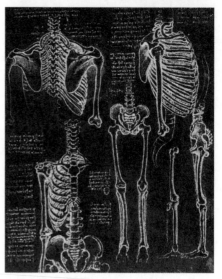

pic.164, 165 sketches

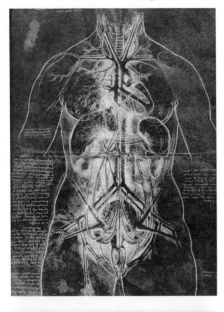

..."By human beings are the muscles, which move the lips, more numerous than by other creatures. This is necessary because of the many activities... ...be it to pronounce the letters b, f, m, p or to whistle, to laugh, to cry or to make curious distortions to imitate grimaces."

..."The act of procreation and the elements, which are used for it, are so abhorrently ugly, that nature would loose the human species, if the faces and affects of the procreationing people and the restrained lust would not have something beautiful in it."

...This child´s heart is not beating and it neither breathes, because it lies continually in water. If it would breathe, it would drown..."

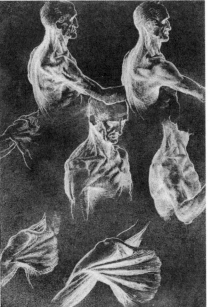

pic.166, 167 sketches

physiology

architecture

Leonardo was planning the „ideal city" with different levels for supply and disposal infrastructure, as well as layers for the different social classes. He concerned himself with domed structures for churches, with fortifications as well as with the planning of private residential houses. With a specificity of great attention he concentrated on the arch as a building element.

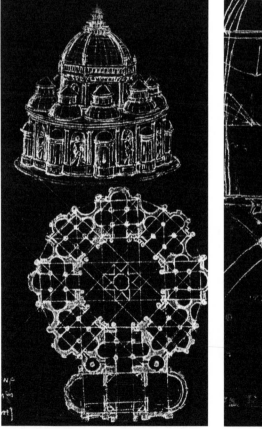

..."A building has to stand alone, because it should show its true stature."

..."Where as in the pantry, the entry to the kitchen has to be in its back, to fulfill its work briskly, and the window of the kitchen has to be positioned on the front side of the pantry, to get wood."

..."An arch is nothing else than a strength, which is bred by two weaknesses..."

..."By a church you should not see the roofs, they should be planned flat and through gutters the water should run into tubes."

pic.168, 169 architectural sketches

pic.170 Archimedes screw

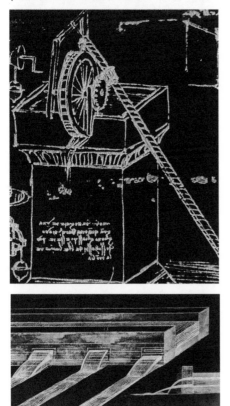

pic.171, 172 sketches of constructions
with water

Leonardo concerned himself with the theme of water in an exceptionally and intensive way and from multiple perspectives: As an explorative, in itself contradictory element, as a force of nature to be tamed, as a potential weapon against the enemy, as an alignment, indispensable to life, which has to be utilized, to the point of the planning of hydraulic constructions or a bathroom for the dutchess.

…"The water removes mountains and fills the valley and would make the earth completely spherical, if it could do this."

…"The seaweed, the grass, which grows on the seabed, does not bend and is not pressed on the ground, but permeates the water like it would grow in the air. Out of this I draw the conclusion, that all elements do not have weight in their own sphere."

…"If 12 ounces of water can make a mill stone rotating 30,000 times in an hour, I believe, that 24 ounces could make a mill stone rotate 60,000 times and he will grind double that much as before."

…"The water wheel will be turned better, if the water, which it turns, does not spring back after the impact."

water

Leonardo as a drawer

..."The painter has to learn first the perspective, then the measurements of all things, then the hand of a great master , to accustom himto draw proper extremities, and then according to the nature, to convince him of the reasons for the learned things."

..."Women have to be illustrated in modest gestures, the legs close together, the arms one upon the other, the head drooped and turned to the side."

..."Old broads have to be illustrated ferociously and provocatively, with irate movements, like the characters of infernal furies. Old men with inertial and slow movements, the legs bent by the knees, the back cambered , the head drooped..."

pic. 173 sketch of a foundry
of cannons

abb. 174 The Last Supper

abb.175 Mona Lisa

..."The painting contains all ten fields of a face, namely the dark, light, the character of the bodies and colour, shape and position, the distance and closeness, movement and composure."

..."Observe the faces of men and women, on the streets when it is getting dark and the weather is bad, how much gracefullness and blandness you can see on it."

..."Colours loose their nature the same way, like bodies loose their dimension with distance."

Leonardo as a painter

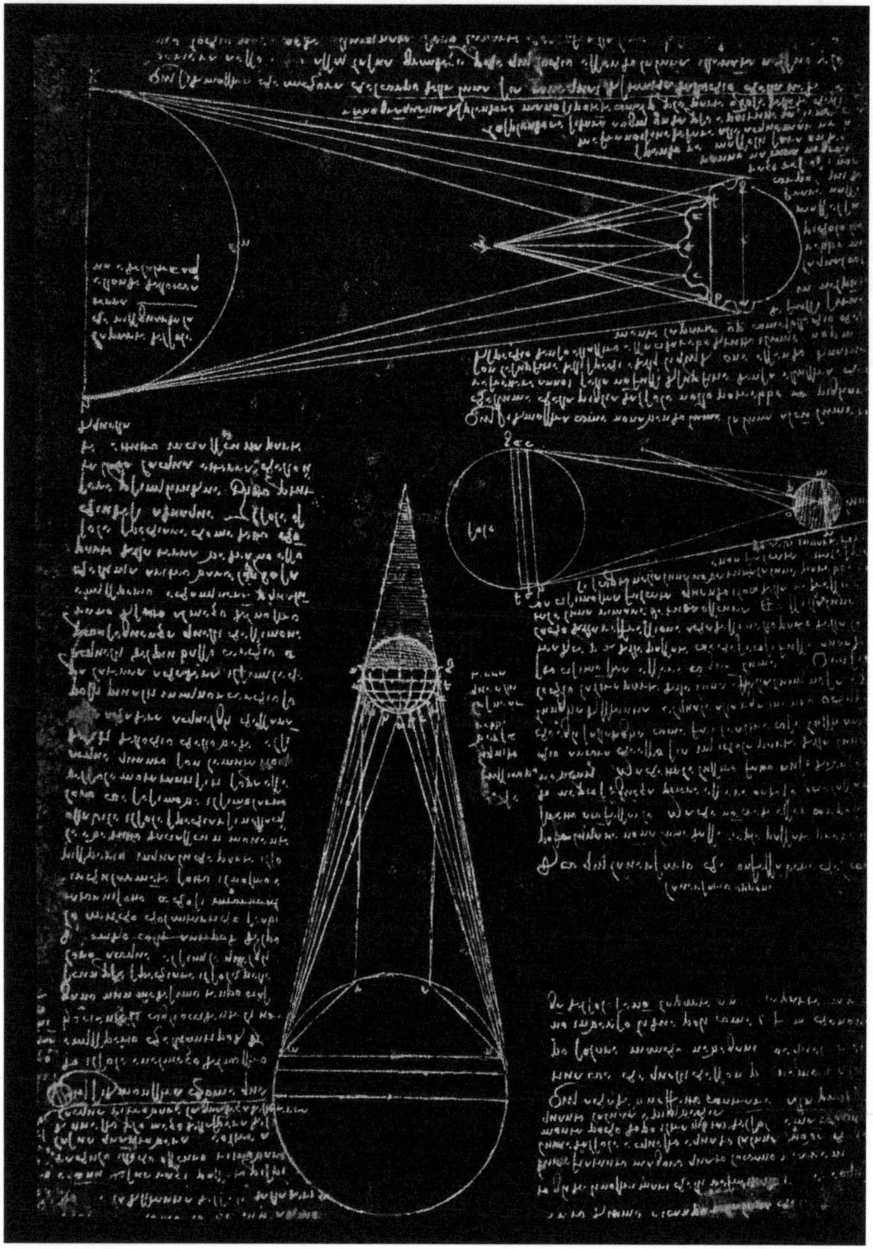

astronomy

pic.176 sketch

"Each month the moon has once winter and once summer. He has also higher degrees of cold and higher degrees of heat, and the equinoxes are colder then ours."

..."Don magnifying-glasses to see the moon better."

..."The sun has figure, shape, movement, glow, heat and recreating power and all these properties emanate from her, without which she is getting smaller."

..."The sun does not move."

..."The borders of the moon are lighter and appear brighter, because there just the wave peaks of his waters are silhouetted."

..."If you observe the colors constantly, you will find huge differences among them. That comes from clouds, which arise from the waters of the moon and come between the sun and these waters."

..."I divided the disquisition on birds into four books. The first of them is about the flight with wing beat, the second from the flight without wing beat by advantageous winds, the third from the flight in general like those from birds, bats, fish and insects, the last one from the makeshift movement."

...The question about the flight of birds concerned him all his life time. His observations he recorded in innumerable sketches. Thereby he solved the essential "mysteries" of the success in the movement of birds and based his constructions of flight machines on these conclusions.

"You have to anatomically study the wing of a bird together with the muscle of the breast, the movements of these wings."

"The tail increases or decreases the weight of the bird."

"The bird, who is paddling with one wing more than with the other, will move in a circular path."

flight of birds

pic.177,178,179 sketches concerning the bird`s flight

flight of birds

...Leonardo probably gained a good musical expertise. Within the areas of art, after painting, he attributed the highest ranking to music, calling music the „materialization of the invisible". However, he was unpleased with music's transitoriness. Leonardo was able to write scores and was an excellent player of the lyra, obtaining high recognition in public. But he found fault in their transient nature. Leonardo could write the notation, he was an excellent player on the Lyra and obtained general acceptance with his music. With the development of musical instruments he often drew from his other experiences, which were related to his research of human anatomy.

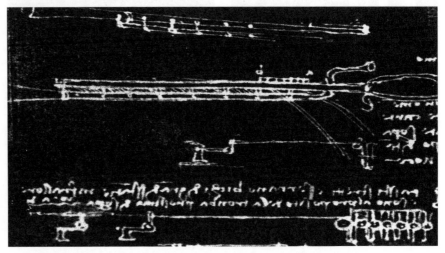

pic.180 sketches concerning the production of musical instruments

"The same bell seems like four bells. She is beaten by two hammers and can switch the voice like the organs."

"These two flutes change their note not by jumps like most of the other wind instruments, but like the human voice."
Leonardo

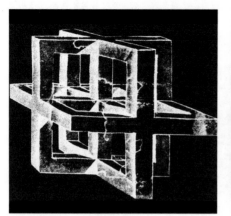

pic.181 geometrical figure

pic.182 geometrical figure

„The point being indivisible, occupies no space. That which occupies no space is nothing."

"Therefore, students, study mathematics and do not build without foundation."

"Every uneven number stays, even if you multiply it with an uneven number, uneven. Every uneven number gets, if you multiply it with an even number, even."

Leonardo

...Leonardo first concerned himself, from the age of 50 on, with methodologies of mathematics.

His interests were focused especially on Euklid and his platonic bodies, Archimedes and his transformation of planes, as well as mathematical means the quadrature of the circle and its proportions. Geometry and mathematics were held as one discipline.

His friend Luca Pacioli, a well known mathematician, assisted him. But for Leonardo, mathematics was principally just means to translate his ideas into practice.

..."It should not read me, who is not after my maxims a mathematician."

..."The span of outstretched arms of a man is equal to his height."

..."I will transform each equilateral body with concurrent sites into a cubic one!..."

..."At first a cylinder is made of it. If you square a rectangular board, which is longer then wide..."

mathematics

... in the night of Saint Andreas I found the end of squaring the circle, when the night and the paper ran out. It was completed by the end of the hour."

..."Archimedes gave in fact the squaring of a multi-sided figure, but not of a circle. Accordingly Archimedes never squared a figure with curved circles. But I am squaring the circle less the smallest part, which the mind can imagine, the visible point."

..."Circles behave to each other just as the squares, which were created by the multiplication of its diameter."

...Leonardo claimed to have resolved the quadrature of a circle. Indeed evidence referring to this could not be found in his notes. Possibly they were lost, like most of his notes. Newer research suggests the Vitruvian man held the resolution to the squaring of a circle. In this study of proportions of the ideal dimensions of a man the encoded mathematical solution to one of the biggest mysteries of mathematics is presumed.

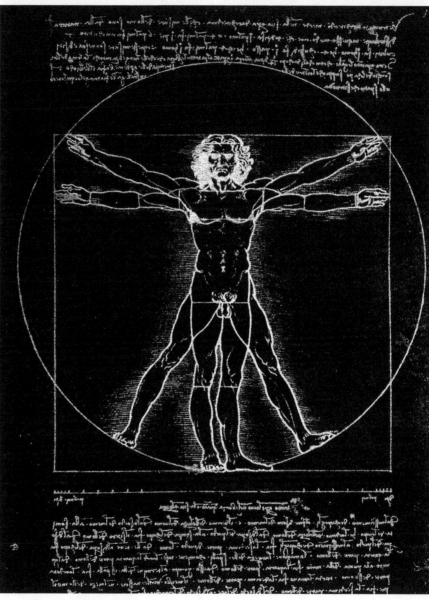

pic.183 „Vitruvian man"

bibliography

Leonardo da Vinci, Eine Biographie in Zeugnissen, Marianne Schneider, Schirmer Mosel Verlag, 2001

Leonardo da Vinci, Gemälde und Schriften, Andre Chastel, Schirmer Mosel Verlag, 2002

Leonardo da Vinci, Das Lebensbild eines Genies, Emil Vollmer Verlag, 1935

Leonardo da Vinci, Tagebücher und Aufzeichnungen, Theodor Lücke, Paul List Verlag, 1940

The Codex Leister by Leonardo da Vinci, Christie Manson & Woods LTD, London, 1980

Leonardo da Vinci, Anatomische Zeichnungen aus der königlichen Bibliothek auf Schloss Windsor, Hamburger Kunsthalle Ausstellungskatalog, Prisma Verlag, 1979

Leonardo da Vinci, Il Codice Atlantico, Giunti Verlag Firenze, 2000

Leonardo da Vinci, Sämtliche Gemälde und Zeichnungen, Frank Zöllner, Taschen Verlag, 2003

Leonardo da Vinci, Mereschkowski, Verlagsbuchhandlung Schulze & Co, Leipzig, 1912

Leonardo da Vinci, Traktat von der Malerei, Verlag Eugen Diederichs, 1909

Galerie grosser Meister - Leonardo, Arnoldo Mondadori Editore, 1975

Leonardo – Das Universalgenie, Alessandra Fregolent, Parthas Verlag, 2002

Leonardo da Vinci und seine Zeit, Robert Wallace, Time Life Verlag, 1966

Leonardo da Vinci, Wissenschafter-Erfinder-Künstler, Otto Letze und T. Buchsteiner, Verlag Gerd Hatje, 2000

Worte Meister Leonardos, Insel-Bücherei Nr.446, Ernst Bertram, Insel Verlag 1950

Lebensläufe der berühmtesten Maler, Bildhauer und Architekten, Giorgio Vasari, Manesse Verlag, 1974

Leonardo da Vinci, Die Aphorismen, Rätsel und Prophezeiungen, M. Schneider, Schirmer Mosel Verlag, 2003

Eine Kindheitserinnerung des Leonardo da Vinci, Sigmund Freud, Fischer Taschenbuchverlag, 1995

Ich aber quadriere den Kreis…, Klaus Schröder und Klaus Irle, Waxmann Verlag, 1998

Leonardo da Vinci, Psychoanalytische Notizen zu einem Rätsel, Kurt R.Eissler, DTV-Verlag,1994

Der Nussbaum im Campanile - Leonardo da Vinci, Isolde Rieger, Verlag Renner 1989

Leonardo da Vinci im Spiegel seiner Zeit, Heinz Lüdecke, Rütten Verlag, 1953

Leonardo da Vinci – Das Wasserbuch, Marianne Schneider, Schirmer Mosel Verlag, 1996

Leonardo da Vinci, Der Flug der Vögel, Marianne Schneider, Schirmer Mosel Verlag, 2000

© David-Atelier 34,35,36,37,38,39,42,43,44,45,46,47,48,49,50,51,52,53,54,55,56,57,58,59,60,61,64,65,66, 67,68,70,72,73,74,75,76,77,78,79,81,82,85,86,88,89,90.91,93,94,96,97,98,99,101,102,103, 104,105,106,107,108,109,110,111,112,113,114,115,118,119,120,122,123,125,127,128,129, 130,133,135,136,137,138,139,140,141,142,143,144,145,146,147,148,149,150,151,152,154, 155,156,157,158,159,160,161,162,163,170,

© Reinhard Fink 1,2,3,4,5,7, 9,10,17,18,19,22,26,30,31,32,33

The following illustrations are from a non-copyright protected CD-ROM "5.555 Meisterwerke", published by Tandem Verlag (daughter company of "DIRECTMEDIA Published GmbH, Berlin")
8,11,14,15,16,21,23,24,25,28,29,174,175,

Permission for the publication of the following sketches are generously allowed by Reprint-Verlag-Leipzig „http://www.reprint-verlag-leipzig.de/"www.reprint-verlag-leipzig.de), Dr. Hermann Grothe – Leonardo da Vinci als Ingenieur und Philosoph – 1874
13, 20, 27, 69, 80, 83, 84, 87, 100, 111, 112, 121, 127

Archive of the author and the publisher:

6,12,13,20,27,40,41,62,63,69,71,80,83,84,87,92,95,100,116,117,121,124,126,128,131,132 ,134,153,164,165,166,167,168,169,171,172,173,176,177,178,179,180,181,182,183,

Credits

Lindauer Druckerei
ESCHBAUMER GmbH & Co

Specialiced partner
for noble and sophisticated products

with love for the detail

quality in completion

flexibility

everything from a hand

consultation	dpt
concept	print
design	finishing

Heuriedweg 37 · 88131 Lindau · Germany
Phone 00 49/83 82/96 30-0 · Fax 00 49/83 82/96 30-90
www.lindauerdruckerei.de